T0298801

Competition or Co-operation? South African and Migrant Entrepreneurs in Johannesburg

Sally Peberdy

SAMP MIGRATION POLICY SERIES NO. 75

Series Editor: Prof. Jonathan Crush

Southern African Migration Programme (SAMP)
2017

AUTHOR

Sally Peberdy is Senior Researcher, Gauteng City-Region Observatory (GCRO). The GCRO is a partnership between the Gauteng Provincial Government, the University of Johannesburg and the University of the Witwatersrand.

ACKNOWLEDGEMENTS

SAMP and its partners in the Growing Informal Cities Project would like to thank the International Development Research Centre (IDRC) for funding the project and this publication. The survey of 928 international and South African migrant informal businesses in Johannesburg was funded by the IDRC and the Gauteng City-Region Observatory.

Published by the Southern African Migration Programme, International Migration Research Centre, Balsillie School of International Affairs, Waterloo, Ontario, Canada, and the African Centre for Cities, University of Cape Town, Cape Town, South Africa

First published 2017

ISBN 978-1-920596-30-9

Cover photo: Sapa/Werner Beukes

Production by Bronwen Dachs Muller, Cape Town

Printed by Print on Demand, Cape Town

CONTENTS

LIST OF TABLES

LIST OF FIGURES

EXECUTIVE SUMMARY

International migrant business owners in South Africa's informal sector are, and have been for many years, the target of xenophobic attacks. This has led to public debates about their role in the South African economy and competition with their South African counterparts, with allegations including that they force the closure of South African businesses, harbour 'trade secrets' that give them the edge, and dominate the sector. As a result, at national government level there has been increasing interest in curtailing the rights of international migrants, particularly asylum seekers and refugees, to run informal enterprises.

This report explores the experiences of 928 international and South African migrant entrepreneurs operating informal sector businesses in Johannesburg. It compares their experiences, challenging some commonly held opinions in the process. The report compares each group, what kind of businesses they operate, and where they do business. It investigates their motivations for migration, employment and entrepreneurial experience prior to and after migration, as well as their motivations for setting up their businesses. It goes on to examine how they set up their businesses, rates of business growth, contributions to local and household economies, and challenges faced, before looking at various interactions between South African and international migrant entrepreneurs in the informal sector of Johannesburg. The main findings are as follows:

- The informal sector in Johannesburg is large and its full extent is unknown. However, the representative Gauteng City-Region Observatory Quality of Life Survey 2015 found that of the 9.6% of respondents who owned a business in the city, 59% operated in the informal sector. Challenging allegations that the sector is dominated by international migrants, only 19% of informal sector business owners in Johannesburg were international migrants. The remainder were migrants from another South African province (25%) or were born in Gauteng (56%).[1]

- International migrants were mostly men (70%), while South African men were slightly over-represented (58%). The overwhelming majority in both groups were black Africans and most were between 25 and 45 years old. South Africans showed higher levels of education with few having had no formal schooling and a significantly higher proportion with completed secondary school and tertiary education. The majority of international migrants were from Southern African Development Community (SADC) countries (65%) or the rest of Africa outside the SADC (22%). The largest cohort of

South African migrants came from Limpopo (25%), Mpumalanga and KwaZulu-Natal (18% each).

- The overwhelming majority of all participants had migrated to provide for their family. South Africans were more likely to have wanted to look for a formal job (82% versus 67% of international migrants). However, they were also more likely to have intended to start their own business (52% versus 40%). Although it is often thought that international migrants have more entrepreneurial experience than their South African counterparts, this was the first business endeavour for the majority of both groups. Only 5% of international migrants and 1% of South Africans had run an informal business prior to migrating and 13% and 5% another informal business since arriving in Johannesburg.

- Informal sector enterprises and entrepreneurs are often seen as survivalist – driven by necessity into starting a business. Yet there are multiple reasons, including entrepreneurial, why people start businesses and the availability of social capital may enable these ambitions. Others seek social recognition and some have altruistic motivations. The survey asked interviewees to rate a series of statements that might have influenced their decision to start a business and an average weight for each factor was calculated. The factors were then grouped and an average score calculated for each category. There was little difference between the scores of South African and international migrants. Although wanting to give their families greater financial security was the strongest motivator for both groups, survivalist reasons/financial benefits and security did not score highest (3.6 for international migrants and 3.7 for South Africans). The category of entrepreneurial orientation/intrinsic rewards scored highest for both (4.2 for South Africans and 4.1 for international migrants). Both groups scored 2.8 in the category of social capital/altruism/status, while South Africans were more concerned with employment considerations (2.6 versus 2.3).

- For both groups of migrants there was a time lag between arrival in Johannesburg and starting their businesses, indicating that most had engaged in other economic activities before getting started.

- There were differences in the types of businesses pursued. The type of business may influence or be influenced by the amount of start-up capital needed, existing skills, profitability and scope for expansion. International migrants (59%) were more likely to be engaged in retail and wholesale trade than South Africans (45%). South Africans were more likely to provide services (53%) than international migrants (30%), while international migrants were more likely to make or manufacture goods (12%) than South Africans (2%). South Africans in the retail sector focused on selling food, particularly fresh fruit and vegetables and cooked food. International migrants focused on other aspects of retail trade.

- Most relied on personal savings to start their businesses (85% of international migrants and 90% of South Africans). Only 4% of South African and 2% of international migrants had secured a loan from a bank. International migrants were more likely to draw on social capital as 25% (compared to 13% of South Africans) started their business with people from their hometown or family, and 24% had secured a loan for start-up capital from relatives compared to 19% of South Africans.

- Amounts of start-up capital were low. South Africans were more likely to start with smaller amounts and 82% compared to 60% of international migrants started with ZAR10,000 or less. International migrants were more likely to have used between ZAR10,001 and ZAR20,000 (20% compared to 13%) and over ZAR20,000 (21% compared to 4%). The amount of start-up capital used can influence the success as well as the type of the business.

- Indicators of business success are profits and growth. Profits are affected by the type of business pursued, the amount of start-up capital used and re-investment in the business. The profits of most (86% of South Africans and 72% of international migrants) fell below the personal and small business income tax thresholds set by the South African Revenue Services (SARS) for the year in question. The average monthly profit after business deductions was ZAR2,000 or less for 35% of South Africans and 25% of international migrants. And 81% of South Africans had net monthly profits of ZAR5,000 or less, compared to 66% of international migrants. However, the incomes of these entrepreneurs, including South Africans, compared relatively favourably with black African incomes in Johannesburg and Gauteng province as a whole.

- The difference between the amount of start-up capital and the current value of the business was used to investigate business growth. There was evidence of growth even at the low end. So, although 19% of international and 24% of South African migrants said the current value of their business was ZAR5,000 or less, double the proportion had used

ZAR5,000 or less in start-up capital. Overall, there was less growth in South African businesses; however, those who had started their businesses with higher amounts of capital grew their businesses at a similar rate to international migrants. Thus, initial capital investment and re-investment of profits rather than nationality may be key to understanding the success of informal businesses. The type of business pursued may also influence how much and how fast a business can grow.

- Informal businesses are often seen as separate from or in competition with the formal sector and as separate from the tax system. The overwhelming majority of participants, regardless of nationality, sourced supplies from formal sector outlets such as wholesalers, factories, supermarkets and the Johannesburg Fresh Produce Market where they are charged VAT. Thus they contribute to the tax base and formal sector profits. South Africans were more likely to buy from supermarkets and small shops, which are likely to charge higher prices that can cut into profits.

- The informal sector entrepreneurs in this survey provided a total of 1,926 full or part-time jobs for others. International migrants (43%) were more likely than South Africns to provide employment to others. Comparing those in both groups who did provide jobs, international migrants provided almost twice as many job opportunities as South Africans: six per business compared to three. South Africans were more likely to employ family members (40% of employers and 25% of employees) compared to international migrants (30% of employers and 23% of employees). Over a third of international migrant enterprises (35%) employed South Africans. In total, 42% (503 people) of non-family employees of international migrants were South Africans.

- Informal sector entrepreneurs contribute to local economies through renting business premises and some derive additional income through renting premises to others. South Africans were slightly more likely to own or be part-owners of their business premises (24% versus 21% of international migrants). They were also more likely to occupy premises without paying rent (45% versus 22%). International migrants were more likely to rent premises from a South African company or individual and pay more rent than South Africans. Some 53% of the South Africans interviewed rented business premises to international migrant entrepreneurs.

- Sending remittances home affects the amount of money that can be re-invested in the business. As many as 31% of international migrants and 17% of South Africans did not remit. Among those who did, South Africans were more likely to remit money once a month or more (44% versus 18%). There was relatively little difference in the amounts remitted each year. However, as South Africans had lower profit margins, remittances could be a bigger drain on their resources. Remittances were mainly used for daily household expenses. Only a few used remittances for savings, investments or to purchase assets.

- Business-related challenges were common, with competition a problem for most. South Africans (43%) were more aware than international migrants (24%) of competition from supermarkets and large stores. Lack of access to credit was a problem for 58% of international migrants and 37% of South Africans. As many as 57% of South Africans and 46% of international migrants said lack of training in business skills was never a problem.

- The informal sector is often seen as standing outside the remit of the state, yet participants in the informal sector have constant interactions with government at national, provincial and municipal levels. While these interactions should be straightforward, both groups had very negative experiences. Around a third of both groups said their goods had been confiscated often or sometimes. In some cases this could be for legitimate reasons. Some interviewees, or their employees, had been arrested or detained (14% of South Africans and 18% of international migrants). Most disturbing were their interactions with police officers. Almost equal proportions (29% of South Africans and 30% of international migrants) had experienced harassment and demands for bribes often or sometimes. As many as 15% of South Africans and 19% of international migrants said they were physically attacked or assaulted by the police often or sometimes.

- Both groups were similarly likely to face crime and conflict with other entrepreneurs. However, international migrants were more likely to experience verbal insults against their business (46% versus 39%), physical assaults by South Africans (24% versus 11%), prejudice against their nationality (55% versus 26%) and gender (39% versus 26%). Some 20% of international migrants said xenophobia had affected their business to some extent. Possibly reflecting interactions between South African and international migrant enterprises, 7% of South Africans said xenophobia had also affected their business.

- South African and international migrant entrepreneurs encounter each other in multiple ways. Almost half of the South Africans (47%) sourced supplies from an immigrant business, 51% had learnt from immigrant businesses and 53% rented business premises to an immigrant business. Over half of the South Africans (52%) said that they had good relations with nearby immigrant business people, 33% felt international migrants have as much right to trade and provide services as South Africans, and 38% agreed that South African and international migrant entrepreneurs can work alongside each other.

- Nearly half of South Africans (48%) thought the number of immigrant-owned businesses should be limited, and 39% that all immigrant businesses should be closed down. However, these negative sentiments may reflect general levels of hostility to international migrants rather than their status as entrepreneurs. The opinions and experiences of South African migrant entrepreneurs show the complexity of attitudes and interactions and that South African entrepreneurs do not speak with one voice.

This survey challenges many widespread opinions about informal sector entrepreneurship in the city and how South African and international migrant entrepreneurs establish and run their businesses. It shows that participation in the informal sector does not necessarily put people in a marginal economic position. It indicates that the success of informal sector enterprises is complex and likely to be related more to start-up capital, the type of business pursued, and re-investment of capital than to nationality. It shows that many if not most of the challenges and problems entrepreneurs face are shared by international migrants and South Africans. This suggests that it would be more fruitful to look at their common problems and identify where best practices could enable them to develop profitable businesses that employ more people and contribute to the development of the city.

INTRODUCTION

Johannesburg in 2015 saw widespread attacks on international migrant businesses, mostly in the informal sector. Although international migrant businesses and their owners have been for many years, and still are, the targets of xenophobia in South Africa, the violence of 2015 led to renewed public debate about their place in South Africa.[2] Attacks on international migrant entrepreneurs largely originate in the communities where their businesses are located. But the South African state has also challenged in court and other arenas the right of international migrants, asylum seekers and refugees to operate small and informal businesses. In 2012, for example, the Limpopo provincial government charged Somali and Ethiopian asylum seekers and refugees with illegally trading and operating businesses. In the subsequent court challenge in the North Gauteng High Court in 2013, the provincial government was joined by the South African Police Services (SAPS), the Department of Home Affairs, the Department of Labour, and two municipal governments. The court upheld the rights of asylum seekers and refugees to operate businesses in South Africa, a judgment confirmed when it was taken to the Supreme Court of Appeal in 2014.[3]

At national government level, there is increasing agreement that the ability of migrant entrepreneurs to operate in the informal sector should be curtailed. Various policy documents and proposed legislation challenge the right and ability of non-nationals, particularly asylum seekers and refugees, to run businesses. These include the Licensing of Businesses Bill (2013), the Immigration Regulations (2014) applying to the amended Immigration Act of 2002, and the Refugees Amendment Bill (2015). The 2016 Green Paper on International Migration proposes that asylum seekers be detained in camps until their claims are approved, and as a consequence they will no longer have the right to run businesses, work or study.[4] The Department of Trade and Industry (DTI), instituted a reference group in 2012 to develop a National Informal Business Development Strategy that was published in 2013.[5] The document devotes a section to the "influx of foreigners into the informal business sector and ensuing conflict with locals."[6] It states that the "gap between the DTI and Home Affairs (in devising strategies and policies to control foreign business activity) especially asylum seekers and refugees was said to have compromised the successes of the informal sector," although it was not made clear which successes it was referring to or how this had supposedly occurred.[7]

In 2013, the then Deputy Minister of Trade and Industry, Elizabeth Thabete, seemed to make her position clear when she claimed that "the scourge of South Africans in townships selling and renting their businesses to foreigners unfortunately does not assist us as government in our efforts to support and grow these informal businesses." She went on to say that "you still find many spaza shops with African names, but when you go in to buy you find your Mohammeds and most of them are not even registered."[8] In 2014, a Department of Small Business Development was created to identify a strategy to manage the informal sector and encourage small, medium and micro enterprise (SMME) development. The Minister, Lindiwe Zulu, acknowledged how apartheid, in restricting black South Africans' rights to move, trade and start businesses, had left many potential entrepreneurs without the institutional memory on which to build their businesses. Initially she acknowledged the right of international migrants to operate businesses saying, "They must make a living. The more they make a living, the more they contribute to the economy. They pay taxes and are active participants in the economy."[9] By 2015 she had changed her tune, arguing that "foreigners" could not expect to co-exist peacefully with others without revealing "trade secrets"; and that they could not "barricade themselves in and not share their practices with local business owners."[10] Similar criticisms were made by the co-chair of the Parliamentary Committee on Home Affairs investigating the xenophobic attacks in early 2015, who essentially blamed the victims for the attacks saying, "they roam, they go to townships to occupy the economic space. We never invaded economic space in exile."[11] The Inter-Ministerial Committee set up to probe the violence referred to the "business models used by migrants to discourage competition such as forming monopolies, evading taxes, avoiding customs and selling illegal and expired goods."

The approach of the municipal government of the City of Johannesburg to the informal sector has been inconsistent.[12] Its focus has been on street traders operating in the central business district (CBD) and inner city but it sometimes acts against traders operating elsewhere. On 30 September 2013, the mayor launched 'Operation Clean Sweep' in Johannesburg, which involved the South African Police Services (SAPS), the Johannesburg Metropolitan Police Department (JMPD), the Johannesburg Roads Agency, City Power (electricity), Pikitup (rubbish collection and street cleaning), Johannesburg Water, the Metro Trading Company, the Department of Home Affairs and the South African Revenue Services (customs and excise). Amid allegations of physical and verbal abuse, the month-long operation swept traders off the streets regardless of nationality, even those who were selling from stands erected by the City and which were being rented from the City.[13] Some shop owners and traders operating from buildings were also affected.[14] The operation removed (at least temporarily) between 6,000 and 8,000 traders from the streets of the CBD and inner city.[15]

This report presents the results of a survey of 928 international and South African migrant informal businesses in the City of Johannesburg conducted by the Growing Informal Cities Project, a collaboration between the Southern African Migration Programme (SAMP), the African Centre for Cities at the University of Cape Town, the Gauteng City-Region Observatory (GCRO) and Eduardo Mondlane University. The survey focused on when and how international migrant entrepreneurs and South African entrepreneurs established their businesses, how their businesses are run, the challenges they face and their contributions to the city. The report systematically compares the two groups of entrepreneurs to address the question of whether or not South Africans are negatively affected by the activities of non-South African entrepreneurs and in the process identifies their shared problems and multiple interactions.

JOHANNESBURG'S INFORMAL ECONOMY

Johannesburg has the largest number of international and internal migrants of any metropolitan area in South Africa (Figure 1). The 2011 Census found that only 53% of the population of the city was born in the province of Gauteng.[16] Over a third of the residents (34% or almost 1.5 million people) were internal migrants born in other provinces of South Africa. Another 13% (or 560,000 people) were born outside South Africa, the largest proportion of international migrants of any major metropolitan area.

The extent of informal sector entrepreneurial activity, by its nature, can never be fully known. However, Statistics South Africa (StatsSA) calculated that in 2013 it contributed ZAR120 billion or 5% to the national GDP.[17] The StatsSA Survey of Employers and the Self-Employed (SESE) in 2013 calculated that nationally 1,517,000 people (45% men and 55% women) were running at least one informal business.[18] It also found that 5% of Gauteng residents of working age had informal businesses (the province with the highest proportion of 6.3% was Limpopo). The report noted that the sector was changing and that, while it had been mainly trading based, construction, manufacturing and finance were "creeping into the sector."[19]

Figure 1: Migrant and Non-Migrant Population of Major South African Metropolitan Areas

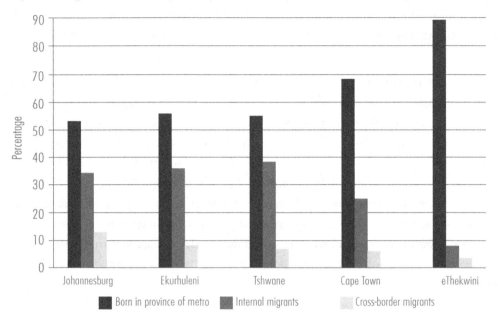

Source: Statistics South Africa (StatsSA) Census 2011

There is no data on the number of people operating informal businesses in Johannesburg. However, a randomized and representative GCRO quality of life survey of Gauteng in 2015 (QoL 2015) included 10,959 Johannesburg residents.[20] It found that 9.6% owned a business, with 59% of these in the informal sector. There were differences by race and sex with 72% of black African, 50% of coloured, 35% of Indian and 31% of white business owners operating in the informal sector. Only 44% of informal sector business owners were women. However, women who owned businesses were more likely to be in the informal sector than men (63% compared to 57%). QoL 2013 asked how residents used the informal sector and found that it had been used by 64% of Johannesburg residents in the previous year. The most common items or services bought or used were food (by 93%), hair salons and barbers (32%), clothes (23%), tailors, sewing and shoe repairs (18%) and accessories (17%). The most common reasons given for using the sector were affordability (mentioned by 72%) and convenience (19%).[21]

Informal sector entrepreneurship ranges from small survivalist businesses to enterprises employing relatively large numbers of people. In Johannesburg, activities include selling bubble gum, sweets and chips; fruit and vegetable stands; small grocery shops and street stalls selling cooked foods. Others sell clothes and shoes (new, used and made by the vendor), accessories, cosmetics and other beauty products. Some sell books, DVDs and CDs, hardware, electrical goods, soft furnishings, furniture, art and sculptures. Entrepreneurs also provide services including hairdressing, and fix and make shoes and clothes. Technologically-savvy individuals have businesses selling and repairing cell phones and providing computer and internet services. Others repair cars and provide welding services. Some operators manufacture goods like metal gates and furniture, make arts and crafts, or run construction or artisanal businesses. Businesses are run on the street, inside buildings (sometimes multi-storey), from yards, garages and houses, road junctions and traffic lights and door- to-door. In Johannesburg, it would be possible to meet a typical household's daily needs entirely from the informal sector.

Policy debates around the presence of international migrant entrepreneurs in the city have heard that international migrant entrepreneurs have "taken over" or dominate the informal sector, particularly in townships. Yet, QoL 2015 found that only 19% of those who owned a business in the informal sector in Johannesburg were international migrants. This means that nearly 80% were South Africans, either from another province (25%) or born in Gauteng (56%). QoL 2015 did find that international migrants (18%) were more likely than internal migrants (9%) or the Gauteng-born (9%) to own a business.[22]

METHODOLOGY

In this study, a migrant entrepreneur is someone who was born outside Johannesburg and moved to the city from another country or place in South Africa including elsewhere in Gauteng. People from outside South Africa are referred to interchangeably as international migrants and immigrants, although some are asylum seekers and refugees. People from elsewhere in South Africa are referred to in this report as internal or South African migrants. The research methodology was developed collaboratively by researchers from the partners in the Growing Informal Cities Project. The original scope of the survey was to interview only international migrant entrepreneurs in Johannesburg and Cape Town.[23] When funds became available the survey was extended to include South Africans in Johannesburg and some questions were modified and others added.[24] A Johannesburg service provider, Quest Research Services (QRS), administered the questionnaire. The interviews were conducted using tablets that allowed the GPS coordinates of the interviews to be captured.

International and South African migrants were interviewed in the same places. These included different types of settlements in the city including the central business district (CBD), inner city residential areas, townships and informal settlements (Table 1). Locations within each were chosen where informal businesses were known to operate. Once the location was selected, interviewers used intervals to randomly select interviewees. Potential interviewees were screened as to eligibility by citizenship, whether they owned the business, and whether it was informal. A business was counted as informal if it was not registered for VAT and had a turnover of less than ZAR1 million per annum in the 2014/2015 tax year. The South African Revenue Services (SARS) and Statistics South Africa (StatsSA) use the additional requirement that a business has less than five employees to be counted as informal.[25] This criterion was not used in this study as the aim was to gather as much information about the employment practices of this cohort of entrepreneurs in the informal economy of the city.

Table 1: Location of Interviews

Location	International (%)	South African (%)
Alexandra	12	6
Chris Hani Baragwanath Hospital	8	5
Bellevue	7	2
Berea	4	3
Brixton	2	3
Chiawelo	4	7
Diepkloof	3	3
Ebony Park	0	3
Hillbrow	4	3
Johannesburg CBD	10	21
Lenasia	3	3
Maponya Mall	4	5
Mayfair	3	3
Orange Farm	2	8
Rosettenville	5	4
Westbury	8	5
Windsor West	2	5

Wynberg	2	4
Yeoville	5	5
Tembisa	1	0
Alexandra and Sandton	6	0
Diepsloot and Midrand	1	0
Ennerdale and Orange Farm	0	0
Greater Soweto	3	0
Randburg and Northcliff	1	0
Roodepoort	0	0

The absence of a pre-existing baseline population database from which to draw a random sample means that it is not possible to guarantee that this is a totally representative sample of international migrant or South African entrepreneurs. However, both sets of interviews were undertaken in the same locations of the city and used the same sampling procedure so comparability is more robust. The original 618 interviews with international migrants were conducted in May 2014. The South African migrant interviews were conducted in October 2014. Funding constraints meant that a smaller number (310) of the latter were interviewed, although statistically valid comparisons can still be made. Mobile entrepreneurs, those working from home, and women entrepreneurs are under-represented as their activities are more difficult to locate. Furthermore, the study did not engage with entrepreneurs in the transport, mining or finance sectors.

PROFILE OF ENTREPRENEURS

The demographic profile of the informal sector entrepreneurs interviewed was diverse, although respondents were overwhelmingly black Africans (Table 2). Reflecting sex ratios in the international migrant population, men significantly outnumbered women among international migrants (70:30) (Table 2). The ratio of male and female South African entrepreneurs was more balanced (58:42). The overwhelming majority of interviewees were aged between 25 and 45 years (Table 2), although international migrants were more likely to be between 20 and 34 years old and South Africans more likely to be over 35 years old. South African migrants had higher levels of education, with fewer having no formal schooling (2% versus 15%), more having completed high school (38% versus 23%) and more with higher education (12% versus 10%) (Table 2).

Table 2: Profiles of Migrant Entrepreneurs

	International (%)	South African (%)
Race		
Black	82.0	96.6
Indian/Asian	11.5	1.9
Coloured/Mixed race	5.5	1.2
White	1.0	0.3
Sex		
Male	70.2	58.2
Female	29.8	41.8
Age		
19 years and under	0.2	0.0
20-24 years	2.6	1.2
25-29 years	18.8	9.3
30-34 years	18.9	17.3
35-39 years	29.9	35.3
40-44 years	18.0	21.4
45-49 years	7.8	9.0
50-54 years	2.3	4.6
55-59 years	1.1	1.5
60+ years	0.5	0.3
Education		
No formal schooling	14.6	1.5
Primary only	14.1	11.5
Some secondary	38.5	37.8
Secondary/high school diploma	23.1	37.5
College certificate/diploma	7.4	10.5
Some/finished university	2.2	1.2

Echoing the cosmopolitanism of Johannesburg, the 618 international migrants in the study came from 27 countries of which 21 were African (Table 3). The majority were from SADC countries (65%), particularly Zimbabwe (30%) and Mozambique (14%). Others were from Nigeria (7%), the DRC, Lesotho and Pakistan (5% each) and India (4%). Respondents born in China, Ethiopia, Malawi, and Somalia comprised only 3% each.

Table 3: Nationalities of International Migrant Entrepreneurs

	No.	%
SADC		
Zimbabwe	186	30.1
Mozambique	89	14.4
DRC	30	4.9
Lesotho	28	4.5
Malawi	20	3.2
Zambia	16	2.6
Swaziland	13	2.1
Angola	11	1.8
Tanzania	7	1.1
East Africa		
Ethiopia	16	2.6
Somalia	16	2.6
Kenya	2	0.3
Eritrea	1	0.2
West Africa		
Nigeria	40	6.5
Cameroon	13	2.1
Ghana	6	1.0
Senegal	1	0.2
Central Africa		
Congo-Brazzaville	12	1.9
Uganda	12	1.9
Rwanda	6	1.0
North Africa		
Egypt	13	2.1
Asia		
Pakistan	28	4.5
India	23	3.7
China	16	2.6
Bangladesh	11	1.8
Europe		
France	1	0.2
Russia	1	0.2

The largest number of South African internal migrant entrepreneurs were from Limpopo (25%) followed by Mpumalanga (18%) and KwaZulu-Natal (18%) (Figure 2). Around 12% were from outside Johannesburg but within the province of Gauteng, and 8% were from the Eastern Cape. The numbers from other provinces were smaller but the data indicates that migrants from throughout South Africa participate in Johannesburg's informal economy.

Figure 2: Place of Origin of South African Migrant Entrepreneurs

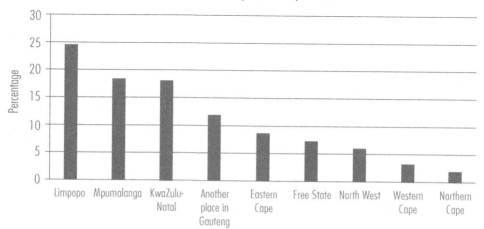

MIGRATING TO JOHANNESBURG

People move for multiple reasons, including to look for economic opportunities and a better life. Some, such as asylum seekers and refugees, migrate because they are forced to. Although racially discriminatory restrictions on international migration to South Africa were ostensibly lifted in 1986, effectively they remained in force until the 1990s.[26] Refugees were not recognized in law until 1998 (and the passage of the Refugees Act which came into effect in 2000), but could gain a form of asylum status from 1993.[27] Although black migrants did move to South Africa before 1994, migration from other African countries (particularly outside the SADC), China and South Asia only commenced in earnest following the demise of apartheid.[28] Similarly, although the control of the apartheid state over internal migration and segregation in cities started to wane by the early 1990s, large-scale internal migration only started after 1994. The city's population grew from 2.3 million in 1991 to 2.6 million in 1996, and then to 3.2 million in 2001 and 4.4 million in 2011.[29]

These historical patterns of movement are reflected in data on when respondents first arrived in Johannesburg (Figure 3). The migration patterns of international and internal migrant entrepreneurs are somewhat similar with both groups dominated by those arriving since 2000. A third of both South African and international migrants arrived between 2000 and 2004 with the next largest cohort of interviewees arriving between 2005 and 2009. Higher rates of arrival among international migrants between 2010 and 2014 reflect the economic crisis in Zimbabwe.

Figure 3: Year of Arrival in Johannesburg

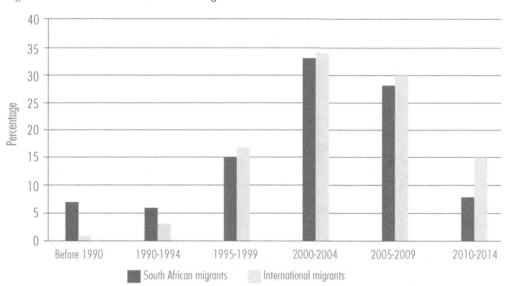

Although it is often said that international migrants arrive with more entrepreneurial experience than their South African counterparts, the occupational profiles of both groups prior to migrating were similar (Table 4). Relatively few in either group had run an informal business before moving to Johannesburg (1% of South Africans and 5% of international migrants). Roughly similar proportions were unemployed before migrating (50% of internal and 56% of international migrants). The same proportions had been students (9%) and unskilled manual workers (8%). That 10% of internal migrants but only 4% of international migrants had been domestic workers reflects the major role of domestic work as an occupation for black women in South Africa.[30] A number of both groups had been professionals, including teachers, health workers and managers.

Table 4: Occupation prior to Migrating

	International (%)	South African (%)
Unemployed/job seeker	55.8	49.8
Scholar/student	8.7	9.4
Manual worker (unskilled)	7.9	7.8
Manual worker (skilled)	4.9	6.8
Domestic worker	3.7	10.0
Office worker	3.7	3.2
Informal sector business (same activity)	3.7	0.6
Self-employed formal business	2.3	1.6
Teacher	1.6	1.0
Agricultural worker	1.6	3.9
Employer/manager	1.0	0.6
Health worker	1.0	1.0
Informal sector business (different activity)	1.0	0.6
Mineworker	0.8	1.9
Professional	0.7	0.0
Police/military/security	0.5	1.3
Traditional healer	0.2	0.3
Other	1.2	0.0

The main intention of most entrepreneurs, regardless of where they came from, was to find a formal job in Johannesburg (67% of international migrants and 82% of South Africans), no doubt with the intention of being able to support their family members (82% of international migrants and 84% of South Africans) (Table 5). While few had entrepreneurial experience, many had entrepreneurial ambitions. Over half of the South Africans intended to start their own business (52%) or join a family business (11%), a higher proportion than among international migrants (40% and 12% respectively). Many in both groups had existing social networks in Johannesburg and had been encouraged to move by friends and relatives (54% of South Africans and 48% of international migrants).

After arriving in Johannesburg, the largest cohorts of international and internal migrants had been unemployed (47% and 41% respectively) (Table 6). The gaps in prior experience grew wider as 13% of international migrants but only 5% of South African migrants said they had operated another informal business since arriving in the city. For the majority of both groups this was their first business endeavour.

Table 5: Reasons for Migrating to South Africa/Johannesburg

	International (% agreed)	South African (% agreed)
I wanted to provide for my family	81.7	83.6
I intended to look for a formal job	67.2	82.4
I was encouraged to come by friends/relatives already here	48.4	54.2
I intended to start my own business	39.5	51.7
I intended to join a family business	11.5	11.1
I intended to further my studies	9.4	25.4
I came as a refugee/asylum seeker	34.0	

Table 6: Occupations since Arriving in Johannesburg

	International (%)	South African (%)
Unemployed/job seeker	47.1	41.4
Manual worker (unskilled)	12.8	11.0
Informal business (same activity)	9.1	3.7
Domestic worker	6.6	12.7
Self-employed formal business	4.5	2.5
Manual worker (skilled)	5.0	9.5
Informal business (different activity)	4.2	1.2
Office worker	1.9	3.4
Scholar/student	2.1	5.6
Agricultural worker	0.8	2.8
Police/military/security	0.8	1.9
Employer/manager	0.7	0.6
Health worker	0.7	0.8
Mine worker	0.3	1.6
Teacher	0.5	0.9
Professional (e.g. lawyer, doctor, academic, engineer)	0.2	0.2
Traditional healer	0.2	0.3
Other	2.8	0.0
Note: Multiple response question		

19

ENTREPRENEURIAL MOTIVATION

Literature on what motivates people to start informal sector businesses largely divides them into survivalists and opportunity-driven entrepreneurs.[31] In general, the literature leans towards survivalist explanations for starting informal businesses.[32] The informal sector is seen as an income-earning opportunity of last resort; the only means of financial survival. However, informal sector entrepreneurs may be drawn to starting their own businesses for more entrepreneurial reasons, such as wanting to be self-employed, feeling that entrepreneurship suits their personality, and that it provides intrinsic rewards unavailable through formal employment. The availability of financial and social capital, in the form of family or friends who can provide support and advice, may also play a role. Others may see possibilities for social recognition or upward social mobility. And for some there may be associated altruistic rewards which, while unlikely to be the prime reason for starting or sustaining a business, may be important in the package of reasons that make up a decision to enter the entrepreneurial arena. In South Africa, studies of the informal sector have uncovered a range of possible reasons for starting an informal business.[33]

This survey asked interviewees to rate a series of statements that might have influenced their decision to start their business on a scale from 1 (no importance) to 5 (extremely important). The factors were drawn from other studies of what propels people into entrepreneurship. A mean score or average weight for each factor was then calculated with a score of 5 demonstrating that the factor was extremely important and 1 that it was of no importance in the decision to start the business (Table 7).[34] The factors were then grouped into four categories and an average score calculated for each category.

Overall, the differences between South African and international migrants were not great. Both felt strongest about wanting to give their families greater financial security (mean score of 4.5 for both groups). However, international migrants felt more strongly about the need to earn money to remit to their families (4.3 compared to 3.9). Both felt strongly about the "need to make more money just to survive". Unemployment and unsuitable employment played less of a role for both, but unemployment was a stronger motivator for South Africans (3.4) than for international migrants (2.5).

Table 7: Entrepreneurial Motivation Scale

	International (%)	South African (%)
Survivalist/financial benefits and security		
I wanted to give my family greater financial security	4.5	4.5
I needed more money just to survive	4.3	4.4
I wanted to make more money to send to my family in my home country/province/town	4.3	3.9
I was unemployed and unable to find a job	2.5	3.4
I had a job but it did not suit my qualifications and experience	2.2	2.1
Mean score	3.6	3.7
Entrepreneurial orientation/intrinsic rewards		
I wanted more control over my own time/to be my own boss	4.4	4.3
I like to challenge myself	4.3	4.4
I have the right personality to run my own business	4.1	4.4
I like to learn new skills	4.1	4.4
I wanted to do something new and challenging	4.1	4.3
I enjoy taking risks	3.9	3.9
I wanted to compete with others and be the best	3.9	3.7
I have always wanted to run my own business	3.9	4.3
Mean score	4.1	4.2
Social capital/altruism/status		
I wanted to increase my status in the community	3.7	3.7
I wanted to contribute to the development of South Africa	3.2	3.7
I had a good idea for a service/product for immigrants	3.0	2.7
I wanted to provide a product/service to South Africans	2.9	3.4
Support and help in starting my business was available from other people from my home country/province/town	2.2	2.0
My family members have always been involved in business	2.2	2.1
I decided to go into business in partnership with others	2.1	2.0
Mean score	2.8	2.8
Employment		
I wanted to provide employment for members of my family	2.9	2.8
I wanted to provide employment for other people from my home country/province/town	2.7	2.3
I wanted to provide employment for South Africans	2.1	2.1
I had a job but it did not pay enough	1.8	2.6
Mean score	2.3	2.6

Notwithstanding the strength of some financial or survivalist related factors, the mean score for this category (3.7 for South Africans and 3.6 for international migrants) was lower than the mean score for the category of entrepreneurial orientation and intrinsic rewards (4.1 and 4.2 respectively). South Africans felt more strongly than international migrants that wanting to run their own business had motivated them to do so (mean score of 4.3 compared to 3.9).

Factors related to social capital, altruism and status were weaker motivators (mean score for both groups was 2.8). However, wanting to increase their status in the community was the strongest motivator in this category (score of 3.7 for both). Employment-related factors were relatively unimportant (average mean score of 2.3 for international migrants and 2.6 for South Africans). Thus, it seems that although both South African and international migrant entrepreneurs were motivated to start their businesses for financial reasons, most also felt that they had the right personal attributes and ambitions to start a business and be successful.

BUSINESS OWNERSHIP

AGE OF BUSINESS

Less than 10% of both South African and international entrepreneurs had established their business before 2000 (Table 8). The majority in both groups started operations after 2004: 79% of South Africans and 73% of international migrants. There is a notable lag between the year of arrival in Johannesburg and the year businesses were established for both international and South African migrants (Table 8). These figures show that the majority had engaged in other economic activities (or tried to) before starting their current business (see Table 7). So, although around one in five South African (23%) and international migrants (20%) arrived in Johannesburg between 1990 and 1999, only 6% and 5% respectively established their businesses in the same decade. A similar story is found in the decade from 2000 to 2010. In part, these disjunctures may reflect the economic downturn in South Africa of the late 2000s, which might have made it more difficult to find and keep employment. Or it could be that respondents were saving to start their own business, as personal funds were found to be the main source of start-up capital.

Table 8: Year of Migrant Arrival and Business Start-Up

	International		South African	
	Year of arrival (%)	Year of start-up (%)	Year of arrival (%)	Year of start-up (%)
Before 1980	0.2	0.0	0.6	0.3
1980-1984	0.2	0.0	3.2	0.0
1985-1989	0.5	0.0	3.5	0.3
1990-1994	3.4	0.6	6.5	1.5
1995-1999	16.5	4.0	16.1	5.0
2000-2004	33.8	21.7	33.2	14.9
2005-2009	30.4	35.0	28.1	32.2
2010-2014	15.0	38.7	8.7	45.8

TYPES OF BUSINESS

Entrepreneurial activity in the informal sector involves more than buying and selling and includes service provision as well as the making and manufacturing of goods. The type of activity pursued may influence, or be influenced by, the amount of capital needed to start the business, existing skills, profitability and scope for expansion. International migrants were more likely to be in retail or to make or manufacture goods than South Africans (Table 9). Over half of the South Africans provided services, but only 30% of international migrants did the same. More than one in 10 international migrants (12%) were involved in manufacturing goods compared to just 2% of South Africans. The picture becomes more complex as some businesses involve more than one activity. For instance, a hair salon owner may also sell hair products and even CDs and DVDs. Spaza shops (similar to corner shops) sell groceries, household goods, toiletries, fresh fruit and vegetables, cigarettes and news-papers. People who make or manufacture goods are likely to sell their products themselves.

Table 9: Type of Enterprise

	International (%)	South African (%)
Retail and wholesale trade	58.6	44.6
Services	29.8	53.3
Make or manufacture goods	11.7	2.2

Food-related products were an important part of retail sales (Table 10). South African migrants (92%) were far more likely to sell food products than international migrants (49%). This applied particularly to fruit and vegetables, cooked food and livestock (Table 10). International migrants (45%) were more likely to sell clothing, shoes, toiletries, cosmetics and accessories than South Africans (28%). Services were dominated by hairdressing, sewing and shoe mending (Table 10). Manufacturing activities included making steel gates, window frames, doors and furniture, as well as welding. Some made arts and crafts, including baskets, and others sewed.

Table 10: Types of Goods and Services Provided

	International (%)	South African (%)
Food retail		
Fresh produce (fruit and vegetables)	12.9	24.8
Cigarettes/sweets/biscuits	10.2	11.0
Confectionary (sweets and cakes)	9.7	10.6
Cooked food – ready to eat	6.1	23.2
Livestock (e.g. chickens)	1.9	5.8
Other food	7.9	6.5
Other retail		
Clothing and footwear	22.5	9.0
Toiletries and cosmetics	13.9	10.6
Household products	12.9	6.5
Accessories (bags, sunglasses etc.)	8.7	8.1
Art and crafts (paintings, beadwork, sculptures)	8.3	4.2
Electronics	7.6	3.2
Music/film CDs/DVDs	5.7	4.2
Newspapers	3.6	3.5
Hardware/tools	3.7	1.6
Furniture	1.6	1.3
Books	0.8	2.3
Medicine (drugs)	0.8	1.3
Services		
Sewing/tailoring	5.2	4.8

Haircutting/hair salon	4.9	7.1
Telephone/airtime	2.1	1.6
Car repairs	1.8	1.0
Shoe repairs	1.6	3.5
IT/internet	1.6	0.3
Traditional medicine/traditional goods	0.5	1.3
Other	1.9	1.8
Note: Multiple response question		

BUSINESS PREMISES

Informal sector entrepreneurs try to locate their businesses where they will find a ready market (Table 11). Most ran their businesses from some sort of permanent structure. South Africans were far more likely to use a temporary or permanent stall located on the street or roadside or at transport nodes (65% compared to 39%). International migrants were more likely to operate their businesses from a shop or workshop, whether stand-alone or in a house/yard or garage or market. Some worked in their own or their customers' homes. Others were more mobile, working door-to-door or from vehicles and caravans (10% of international migrants and 5% of South Africans). The higher proportions of South Africans located in permanent stalls, on the roadside and at transport nodes, suggest better access to sites with more traffic and lower rents. These sites may be less attractive or accessible to international migrants because of exposure to xenophobia and officialdom. Most respondents were fairly settled as only 7% of South African and 3% of international migrants used more than one kind of site while a few were mobile entrepreneurs.

Table 11: Usual Location of Business Premises

	International (%)	South African (%)
Permanent stall in a market	24.8	17.7
Permanent stall on the street/roadside	18.1	31.6
Temporary stall on the street/roadside	17.5	24.8
Workshop or shop	15.5	6.5
Shop in house/yard/garage	10.6	6.1
No fixed location, mobile (e.g. door to door)	7.8	2.9

In own home	3.4	6.1
Taxi rank on side of road	2.8	3.2
Vehicle (car, truck, motor bike, bike)	2.1	0.1
Taxi/public transport station in permanent structure	0.5	5.2
In customer's home (e.g. hairstyling)	0.2	1.0
Note: Multiple response question		

BUSINESS START-UP

Although it might be thought that South Africans would have stronger social networks and capital to call on, they were more likely (83%) than international migrants (70%) to have started their business alone (Table 12). Only a few (16%) had started it with other South Africans, including family members. Demonstrating stronger social networks, international migrants were more likely to have started their business with people from their home country (16%) or family (9%) and even with people from other countries including South Africa (3%).

Table 12: Origins of Business

	International (%)	South African (%)
I started it alone	70.2	83.3
I started it with people from my home town	16.2	5.6
I started it with my family	9.1	7.1
I started it with people from other countries	2.1	0.0
I started it with South African business partners	0.8	3.4
I bought this business from a South African	0.6	0.6
I bought this business from a non-South African	0.3	0.0
Other	0.8	0.0

Access to capital to start their businesses was a problem for most interviewees. Some used just one source, while others used two to four sources. Informal sources dominated. Personal savings were the main source of start-up capital for 80% of South African and 85% of international migrants (Table 13). Social networks were also important. Again, international migrants appeared to have stronger networks as over a quarter (26%) had used a loan from relatives compared to 19% of South Africans. They were also almost as likely as South Africans (8% compared to 9% respectively) to have used a loan from non-relatives. South Africans were more likely to belong to *stokvels* or other informal financial institutions, but also more likely to have used usurers/*mashonisa* (Table 13).[35]

Table 13: Sources of Start-Up Capital

	International (%)	South African (%)
Personal savings	85.1	89.7
Loan from relatives	24.4	18.9
Loan from non-relatives	7.6	8.6
Mashonisa (informal money lenders)	2.9	4.1
Loan from informal financial institutions (e.g. *stokvels*)	2.6	11.0
Bank loan	1.5	4.1
Business credit (goods on terms)	0.6	0.3
Loan from government agency	0.6	0.3
Loan from micro-finance institution	0.0	0.3
Note: Multiple response question		

The formal sector was conspicuous by its absence as a source of start-up capital. Only 4% of South African and 2% of international migrants had obtained start-up capital from a bank loan, although 14% and 9% respectively had applied. For South Africans, the main reasons for rejection were insufficient collateral (54%), incomplete documents (31%) and an enterprise deemed unviable (15%). For international migrants, the reasons cited for refusal were no South African identity document (45%), not South African (17%), incomplete documents (14%), insufficient initial capital (14%) and insufficient collateral (10%). Thus, for international migrants, their nationality is the major obstacle in accessing capital from banks. Access to further operating capital can enable a business to survive a slump or to grow. However, only 7% of both groups had borrowed money for their business operations in the previous 12 months. South Africans were most likely to have received the loan from a bank, relatives or informal financial institutions. International migrants were most likely to have a loan from relatives, informal money lenders and informal financial institutions.

The amount needed to develop a successful enterprise partly depends on the type of business pursued. The informal sector does provide opportunities for entry-level entrepreneurs and people with low levels of savings. But businesses that start with inappropriately low levels of capital tend to struggle to survive. South Africans were more likely than international migrants to have started their businesses with low levels of capital (Figure 4). One in five (20%) international migrants and a quarter (26%) of South African migrants had used ZAR2,500 or less to start their current business (Figure 4). And, 82% of South Africans compared to 60% of international migrants had used ZAR10,000 or less to start their business (Table 17). Conversely, international migrants were likely to have used more start-up capital. Twenty percent had between ZAR10,001 and ZAR20,000 compared to 13% of South Africans. Another 21% had used over ZAR20,000, but only 4% of South Africans had done the same.

It is not clear why international migrants generally had more start-up capital than their South African counterparts. International migrants were more likely than South Africans to access sources of capital beyond personal savings. However, the difference may also reflect the type of business being established. Entrepreneurs in the retail and wholesale trades (where 59% of international and 45% of South African migrants operated) were likely to have used more start-up capital than those in other sectors. Businesses in the services sector (where 30% of international and 53% of South African migrants operated) used the lowest amounts of start-up capital.

Figure 4: Amount of Start-Up Capital

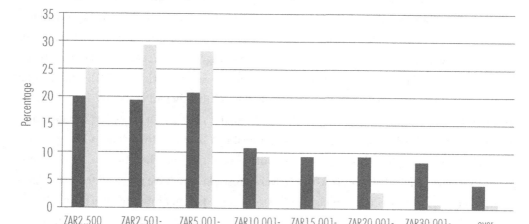

There is a fairly widespread belief that international migrant entrepreneurs have had more opportunity to develop entrepreneurial skills than South Africans. Yet the majority, regardless of nationality, were self-taught (Table 14). South Africans (68%) were more likely to agree than international migrants (56%). International migrants appeared more self-assured with 37% saying they did not need any skills compared to 30% of South Africans. Reflecting the importance of social networks, one in five had learnt from friends and relatives. International migrants were as likely as South Africans (6%) to say they had learnt from previous work experience. Only 4% of international migrants and 3% of South Africans had learnt through on-the-job training. Importantly, given statements by the Minister of Small Business Development demanding international migrant entrepreneurs share their expertise, 51% of South Africans said that they had learnt from immigrant businesses.

Table 14: Skills Acquisition by Entrepreneurs

	International (%)	South African (%)
Self-taught	56.0	68.4
No skills needed	37.4	30.0
Learning from friends and relatives	19.3	19.0
Previous work experience	6.3	5.8
Apprenticeship/on-the-job training	3.7	3.2
University, school or other training centre	3.1	1.3
Training courses/programmes (government)	2.3	0.0
Training courses/programmes (non-governmental including private)	1.8	2.3
Note: Multiple response question		

BUSINESS EXPANSION

The best indicators of business success are net profits and increase in the value of the enterprise. Informal sector entrepreneurship is often associated with marginality, low incomes and tax avoidance. The profits of 86% of South African and 72% of international migrants fell below the personal and small business income tax thresholds set by SARS for 2014/2015 and therefore were not liable for tax.[36]

Overall, and perhaps reflecting the lower levels of capital investment of South African migrants and/or the types of business they pursue, the net monthly profits of South Africans were lower than those of international migrants (Table 15). The average monthly profit after business expense deductions of over a third (35%) of South African and a quarter (25%) of international migrant businesses was ZAR2,000 or less. Income differentials increased as 81% of South Africans declared net monthly profits of ZAR5,000 or less but only 66% of international migrants did the same. Almost a quarter (23%) of international migrants declared monthly profits of ZAR5,001-ZAR10,000 compared to 12% of South Africans.

Table 15: Net Monthly Profit

	International (%)	South African (%)
<ZAR1,000	14.4	12.6
ZAR1,001-ZAR2,000	10.4	22.1
ZAR2,001-ZAR3,000	14.2	17.3
ZAR3,001-ZAR4,000	14.2	17.7
ZAR4,001-ZAR5,000	12.8	11.3
ZAR5,001-ZAR6,000	5.9	4.8
ZAR6,001-ZAR7,000	5.7	4.3
ZAR7,001-ZAR8,000	3.5	0.9
ZAR8,001-ZAR9,000	1.0	0.0
ZAR9,001-ZAR10,000	6.7	2.2
ZAR10,001-ZAR15,000	3.7	2.2
ZAR15,001-ZAR20,000	3.5	1.7
>ZAR20,000	4.0	2.9

Although these incomes may appear low, overall they compare relatively favourably with black African incomes in Johannesburg and Gauteng province as a whole. However, this may say more about the parlous state of the incomes of black African incomes in the province than the informal sector. In 2011, 68% of black African individuals with an income in Johannesburg earned ZAR3,200 or less per month, compared to 41% of international and 47% of South African migrant entrepreneurs in this survey (Table 16).[37] The average monthly net profits of the informal sector entrepreneurs in this survey also compare favourably with black African household incomes in Gauteng in QoL 2015 (Table 16).

Table 16: Comparison of Net Business Profit with Individual and Household Income

	International net monthly business profit 2014 (%)	South African net monthly business profit 2014 (%)	Census 2011 monthly black African *individual* income (Johannesburg) (%)	GCRO QoL 2015 monthly black African *household* income (Gauteng) (%)
<ZAR3,201	41	47	68	57
ZAR3,201-ZAR6,400	32	34	15	20
ZAR6,401-ZAR12,800	16	7	8	12
ZAR12,801-ZAR25,600	8	4	5	8
>ZAR25,600	3	2	3	4

Respondents were asked to estimate the current value of their business including goods, machinery and business premises. Almost a quarter (24%) of South Africans and 19% of international migrants estimated the current value of their business at ZAR5,000 or less (Table 17). Half of South African migrants valued their businesses at ZAR10,000 or less compared to just a third of international migrants. Others had considerable amounts invested in their businesses.

The difference between the amount of start-up capital used and the current value of the business indicates whether businesses are growing or not. Despite seemingly low amounts of start-up capital, and even relatively low current values of businesses for some, there is evidence of growth in these informal businesses, even at the low end. So, although 19% of international and 24% of South African migrants said the current value of their business was ZAR5,000 or less, double the proportion (54% of South African and 39% of international migrants) had used ZAR5,000 or less in start-up capital. For both South African and international migrants, the higher proportions who valued their businesses at over ZAR15,000 than had invested that amount are notable. Only 4% of South African businesses had begun with ZAR20,001 or more in start-up capital and 27% placed the current value of their business at more than ZAR20,000. The equivalent figures for international migrants were 21% and 47%. This suggests that, with the appropriate business and sufficient capital investment, South African entrepreneurs are equally adept as international migrants in growing their businesses. Thus, initial capital investment and subsequent re-investment of profits into the business may be key to understanding the success of informal businesses, not nationality. Furthermore, different types of businesses may require different amounts of start-up capital and deliver different profit margins as well as opportunities for growth.

Table 17: Comparison of Start-Up Capital with Current Value of Business

	International start-up capital (%)	International current value of business (%)	South African start-up capital (%)	South African current value of business (%)
ZAR5,000 or less	38.8	19.3	54.0	24.3
ZAR5,001-ZAR10,000	21.0	13.6	27.8	26.1
ZAR10,001-ZAR15,000	10.6	10.7	8.2	13.6
ZAR15,001-ZAR20,000	9.1	9.2	5.5	9.2
ZAR20,001-ZAR30,000	8.6	13.2	2.7	9.2
ZAR30,001-ZAR50,000	7.9	11.4	1.4	9.2
ZAR50,001-ZAR100,000	2.7	12.7	0.3	6.3
ZAR100,001-ZAR500,000	1.2	8.1	0.0	2.2
ZAR500,000 and above	0.2	1.8	0.0	0.0

ECONOMIC CONTRIBUTIONS

ECONOMIC CONTRIBUTIONS TO THE FORMAL SECTOR

Most informal sector entrepreneurs buy their supplies from formal sector outlets. Table 18 shows the heavy reliance of all entrepreneurs on outlets such as wholesalers, factories, supermarkets, and the Johannesburg Fresh Produce Market. When entrepreneurs buy from the formal sector, they are charged VAT and are thus contributing to the tax base as well as formal sector profits. This challenges preconceptions regarding the contribution of the informal sector to the economy and the tax base. Informal entrepreneurs often use more than one type of outlet to source supplies for their business, with almost a third using at least two sources and others up to five different types of suppliers.

Wholesalers were the major source of supply for entrepreneurs regardless of nationality. International migrants were more likely to buy goods directly from factories (27%

compared to 20% of South Africans). Conversely, South Africans were more likely to get goods from supermarkets (33% compared to 17%), small shops/retailers (17% compared to 8%) and the Johannesburg Fresh Produce Market (34% versus 11%). These outlets are likely to charge higher prices than wholesalers and factories, with negative implications for profitability.

Table 18: Where Supplies Sourced for Business

	International (%)	South African (%)
Wholesalers	41.3	41.3
Direct from factories	26.5	20.0
Supermarkets	17.0	32.9
Johannesburg Fresh Produce Market	11.0	34.2
Make or grow supplies	9.9	7.7
Small shops/retailers	8.3	17.4
Home country	6.1	1.0
Other informal sector producers/retailers	3.7	2.6
Another country	3.4	0.0
Farmers in South Africa	1.1	5.8
Scrapyards	0.3	0.6
Parts manufacturers	0.3	0.3
International migrants	0.0	0.3
China Mall	0.0	0.6
Libraries	0.0	0.3
Forest	0.0	0.6
Note: Multiple response question		

Anecdotally, it is said that international migrant entrepreneurs gain an advantage by buying together to get bulk discounts and competitive retail advantage. However, South African migrant entrepreneurs were more likely (42%) to buy in bulk with others than their international counterparts (35%). Entrepreneur arrangements to gain competitive advantage and lower purchase costs may be more complex than anecdote would suggest. It could be that the larger capitalization of some international migrant businesses enables them individually to access goods at cheaper rates or to negotiate sole-supplier discount deals with wholesalers.

EMPLOYMENT GENERATION

The informal sector entrepreneurs in this survey provided a total of 1,926 full or part-time jobs for others. International migrants were more likely than South African entrepreneurs (43% compared to 35%) to employ people (Table 19). They also employed almost twice as many people if they were employers: 6.0 per business compared to 3.1 per business in the case of South Africans. While South African businesses were more likely to hire people full time, international migrants provided more full-time jobs per enterprise (3.1 versus 2.5).

Table 19: Employment Patterns

	International	South African
No. of businesses providing employment	263	108
% of businesses providing employment	42.6	34.8
No. of full-time jobs	825	271
No. of part-time jobs	761	68
% of full-time jobs	52.0	80.0
% of part-time jobs	48.0	20.0
Total employees	1,586	340
Total employees excluding family members	1,492	297
Employees per business providing employment	6.0	3.1

South African entrepreneurs were more likely to employ family members (40% of employers and 25% of employees) than international migrants (30% of employers and 23% of employees). Again, keeping it close to home, South Africans were more likely to employ non-family members from their home province or town (49% of employers and 27% of employees) than international migrants were to employ people from their home countries (32% of employers and 23% of employees). Over a third of international migrant enterprises (35%) employed South Africans, while 27% employed people from other countries. In total, 42% (503 people) of non-family employees of international migrants were South Africans.

PAYING RENT FOR BUSINESS PREMISES

Informal sector entrepreneurs contribute to local economies and the livelihoods of households and individuals, including South African informal sector entrepreneurs, through the rental of their business premises. South Africans (24%) were slightly more likely than international migrants (21%) to own or be part-owners of their business premises (Table 20). They were significantly more likely to occupy their premises without paying rent (45% compared to 22% of international migrants). International migrants were more likely to pay rent to a private owner (company or individual), whether South African (31% compared to 11% of South Africans) or another nationality (7% compared to 2% of South Africans). Indicating better access to municipal stands, a higher proportion of South Africans (18% compared to 12% of international migrants) paid rent to the City of Johannesburg. Informal sector entrepreneurs also provide business space for rent and over half (53%) of the South African entrepreneurs actually rented premises to international migrant entrepreneurs.

Table 20: Tenure Status of Business Premises

	International (%)	South African (%)
Pay rent to private owner who is South African (company or individual)	31.4	11.0
Owner or part-owner	20.6	23.9
Pay rent to council/municipality	11.7	17.7
Rent-free, squatting	11.5	16.1
Rent-free, with permission	10.2	29.0
Pay rent to private owner who is not South African (company or individual)	7.1	1.6
Share space/premises with others	2.6	0.6
Door to door	3.6	0.0
Other	0.5	0.0

Not only were international migrants more likely to pay rent than their South African counterparts, they were also likely to pay more (Table 21). Of those who paid rent, similar proportions paid less than ZAR500 per month. However, 94% of South Africans paid ZAR1,500 or less per month compared to only 47% of international migrants. International migrants renting from South African private owners (individual or company) were proportionally more likely to pay ZAR1,000 or more per month than those who rented from any other kind of landlord.

Table 21: Monthly Rent Paid for Business Premises

	International (% of rent payers)	South African (% of rent payers)
<ZAR500.00	21.7	22.0
ZAR500-ZAR1,000	16.5	45.0
ZAR1,001-ZAR1,500	8.9	27.0
ZAR1,501-ZAR2,000	6.2	2.0
ZAR2,001-ZAR2,500	7.6	2.0
ZAR2,501-ZAR3,000	7.2	1.0
ZAR3,001-ZAR4,000	8.7	0.0
ZAR4,001-ZAR5,000	5.4	1.0
>ZAR5,000	4.8	0.0

REMITTANCES

The overwhelming majority of all interviewees (85% of South Africans and 82% of international migrants) said their intention on arrival in Johannesburg was to provide for their family. However, as many as 31% of international migrants and 17% of South Africans said that they never sent remittances. Only 44% of South Africans and 18% of international migrants remitted money once a month or more. Others remitted more erratically.

Table 22: Frequency of Remitting

	International (%)	South African (%)
Never	30.7	17.0
At least once a month	18.0	44.0
A few times a year	31.2	27.9
Once a year	12.8	2.5
Occasionally (less than once a year)	6.5	8.0
Don't know	0.8	0.6

Entrepreneurs who remit infrequently may be financially constrained (although the data does not suggest a strong relationship between low incomes and low remittance levels) or they could have weak connections to home. There was a relationship between the migration status of international migrants and remitting as 36% of permanent residents, 38% of refugees and 29% of asylum seekers said that they never remit. The families of these entrepreneurs may be with them or, in the case of refugees and asylum seekers, may be difficult to communicate with. Distance also played a role as nationals of countries furthest away from South Africa were more likely to say that they never send remittances.

Proximity and access to affordable and reliable channels to send money may in part explain higher rates of remitting among South African migrants. Remittances could be a drain on a business as money used for this purpose could otherwise be reinvested to enable business growth. Although South Africans remitted more frequently, there was little difference in the amounts that South African and international migrants had sent home in the previous 12 months (Table 23). But with South Africans making less money from their businesses, this could constitute a higher proportion of their profits.

Table 23: Amount Remitted in Previous 12 Months

	International (% remitters)	South African (% remitters)
ZAR1,000 or less	10.5	7.6
ZAR1,001-ZAR2,500	13.5	21.0
ZAR2,501-ZAR5,000	30.5	28.1
ZAR5,001-ZAR7,500	13.8	16.2
ZAR7,501-ZAR10,000	11.4	13.8
ZAR10,001-ZAR15,000	10.3	11.4
ZAR15,001-ZAR20,000	4.3	1.0
Over ZAR20,000	5.7	1.0

South Africans were far more likely to use formal methods to remit money. As many as 69% of South African migrants used banks compared to only 24% of international migrants (Table 24). Other formal methods, such as money transfer agencies, and informal methods are likely to cost more than internal bank transfers in South Africa.

Table 24: Methods Used to Remit Money Home

	International (% remitters)	South African (% remitters)
With family, friend or co-worker	27.7	18.1
Informal money transfer	25.3	12.7
Through a bank	23.9	68.7
Formal money transfer agency (e.g. Western Union, Money Gram)	23.4	1.9
I take it myself	22.2	40.2
Shoprite	0.0	3.9
Note: Multiple response question		

Remittances were primarily used to meet basic needs, such as food, school fees, medical care, clothing and other day-to-day household expenses (Table 25). Only a few households used remittances for savings or investments or to purchase assets such as property, livestock and agricultural equipment. Even fewer used them to start or run a business.

Table 25: Use of Remittances

	International (% remitters)	South African (% remitters)
Buy food	76.9	86.9
Meet other day-to-day household expenses	37.4	32.4
Pay for education/school fees	36.4	46.3
Buy clothes	33.4	48.3
Pay medical expenses	21.0	8.1
Build, maintain or renovate dwellings	19.6	11.2
Special events	15.9	13.5
Transportation	11.4	12.7
Savings/investments	9.8	11.6
Buy property	4.4	3.1
Purchase livestock	4.2	7.7
Agricultural inputs/equipment	3.5	1.5
Start or run a business	2.8	1.2
Note: Multiple response question		

BUSINESS CHALLENGES

South African and international migrants face many of the same problems, suggesting that working together may help overcome them. Their challenges fell roughly into three categories: business-related, engaging with the state, and engaging with other people.

BUSINESS-RELATED CHALLENGES

Business-related challenges were most commonly experienced (Table 26). Competition was a problem for most. International migrants were more likely to frame the problem in terms of "insufficient sales" and "too few customers" and South Africans more likely to say that there were "too many competitors." South Africans (43%) were more aware than international migrants (24%) of competition from supermarkets and large stores. Lack of business skills can be a challenge but 57% of South Africans and 46% of international migrants never lacked the necessary skills. Lack of access to credit was a problem for 58% of international migrants and over a third of South Africans (37%).

Table 26: Business-Related Challenges

		Often (%)	Sometimes (%)	Never (%)
Insufficient sales	International	10.4	78.8	10.8
	South African	3.7	79.6	16.7
Too few customers	International	12.6	77.2	10.2
	South African	8.4	76.8	14.9
Customers don't pay their debts	International	9.7	30.3	60.0
	South African	8.0	31.6	60.4
Too many competitors	International	30.3	49.2	20.6
	South African	50.2	36.5	13.3
Too much competition from supermarkets/large stores	International	23.5	41.4	35.1
	South African	43.0	36.8	20.1
Suppliers charge too much	International	22.7	56.5	20.9
	South African	26.3	57.0	16.7
Lack of training in accounting, marketing	International	13.3	40.6	46.1
	South African	8.7	34.4	57.0

Storage problems	International	8.3	35.9	55.8
	South African	4.6	22.6	72.8
Lack of access to credit	International	27.0	31.4	41.6
	South African	8.0	30.7	61.3

ENGAGING WITH THE STATE

The informal sector is often seen as standing outside the remit of the state and the laws and by-laws promulgated by government at national, provincial and municipal levels. Yet, participants in the informal sector are in constant interaction with the state as they have to comply with a range of laws, by-laws and other regulations. In Johannesburg, informal businesses regularly engage with municipal law enforcement (JMPD, SAPS, SARS and municipal, provincial and national departments of Home Affairs, Labour, Health and the Environment).

While interactions between the state and informal sector entrepreneurs should be straightforward and benign, they are not. Almost a third of both groups said they had goods confiscated often or sometimes (Table 27). However, in some cases this could be for legitimate reasons such as trading in the wrong place. International migrants (18% compared to 14% of South Africans) were slightly more likely to say that they or their employees had experienced arrest or detention.

Table 27: Problems Related to Engaging with the State

		Often (%)	Sometimes (%)	Never (%)
Confiscation of goods	International	7.8	24.3	68.0
	South African	4.0	29.4	66.6
Harassment/demands for bribes by police	International	8.4	21.7	69.9
	South African	7.1	21.7	71.2
Arrest/detention of self/ employees	International	5.2	12.9	81.9
	South African	1.9	12.1	86.1
Physical attacks/assaults by police	International	4.7	13.9	81.4
	South African	2.2	12.7	85.1

Relationships with the police are of major concern. If informal entrepreneurs are operating illegally, they should be charged instead of harassed or assaulted. Almost equal proportions of South African (29%) and international migrants (30%) had experienced harassment and demands for bribes from police often or sometimes (Table 27). More disturbing is that 15% of South African and 19% of international migrant entrepreneurs said that they were physically attacked or assaulted by the police often or sometimes. South Africans were more likely to be assaulted by the police than by other South Africans (Tables 27 and 28).

Asked about their experience of Operation Clean Sweep in the City of Johannesburg in 2013, South Africans (14%) were more likely than international migrants (10%) to have been affected. Of those who were affected, South Africans (27%) were more likely than international migrants (17%) to have been physically assaulted by officials. A further 26% of South Africans and 46% of international migrants were verbally abused by officials. Thus it seems that both groups of entrepreneurs are more at risk of physical and verbal assault from state officials than they are from other entrepreneurs or members of the public.

ENGAGING WITH OTHERS

Regardless of nationality, some of the challenges faced by informal entrepreneurs relate to their interactions with other people (Table 28). South Africans were more likely to say that conflict with other entrepreneurs was a problem for their businesses. Informal sector entrepreneurs may be particularly vulnerable to crime and theft as they are likely to operate from unprotected premises and run cash businesses. International migrants were more likely (10% compared to 6% of South Africans) to say that they often experienced crime and theft. They were also more likely to have often experienced verbal insults, physical attacks by South Africans, and prejudice against their nationality and gender (Table 28).

Xenophobic attacks and abuse are a constant threat for many international migrant entrepreneurs in Johannesburg. One in five international migrants said xenophobia had affected their business "a great deal" or "to some extent" (Table 29). However, 70% said it had no impact on their business. Some South African migrant entrepreneurs had also been affected by xenophobia. This is because some South African and international migrant informal sector businesses may be linked. For instance, South Africans may supply international migrant businesses or get supplies from them, or rent property to them, so if business is disrupted due to xenophobic violence, South African businesses are also affected.

Table 28: Challenges Engaging with Others

		Often (%)	Sometimes (%)	Never (%)
Conflict with other entrepreneurs	International	4.0	47.2	48.7
	South African	10.8	44.0	45.2
Crime/theft	International	9.9	40.8	49.4
	South African	5.6	42.1	52.3
Verbal insults against your business	International	13.1	32.8	54.0
	South African	9.9	28.8	61.3
Physical attacks/assaults by South Africans	International	5.0	18.9	76.1
	South African	0.9	10.2	88.9
Prejudice against my nationality	International	17.2	37.4	45.5
	South African	8.4	17.6	74.0
Prejudice against my gender	International	15.7	22.8	61.5
	South African	9.0	16.7	74.3

Table 29: Impact of Xenophobia on Businesses

	International (%)	South African (%)
A great deal	13.4	0.0
To some extent	6.5	7.4
Not very much	9.5	12.1
Not at all	69.9	80.5
Don't know	0.6	0.0

INTERACTIONS BETWEEN ENTREPRENEURS

South African and international migrant entrepreneurs encounter each other on a regular basis as competitors, within the supply chains of different sectors, as neighbours, and as landlords and tenants. Many South African informal sector businesses have strong symbiotic economic links to those of international migrants (Table 30). Almost half of South Africans (47%) sourced supplies for their businesses from immigrants, over half (51%) had learnt from immigrant businesses and 53% rented business premises to an immigrant business.

Table 30: Relationships between South African and International Migrant Entrepreneurs

	Agree (%)	Disagree (%)	Don't know (%)
I rent business premises to an immigrant business	52.9	47.1	n/a
I have learnt from immigrant businesses	51.4	48.6	n/a
I have good relationships with the immigrant business people near me	51.7	48.3	n/a
I get goods for my business from immigrant business people/businesses	47.1	52.9	n/a
Only a specified number of immigrant-owned businesses should be allowed to trade in this area	48.0	52.0	n/a
South Africans cannot compete with immigrant businesses	37.5	31.0	31.6
Immigrant business people work harder than South Africans	32.5	35.9	31.6
All immigrant-owned businesses should be closed down	38.7	31.3	30.0
It is OK that people loot and burn down immigrant-owned businesses	0.0	100.0	0.0
South African and immigrant business people can work alongside each other	38.4	31.6	30.0
Immigrant business people have just as much right to trade and provide services as South Africans	33.4	35.3	31.3

Many South African migrant entrepreneurs held positive attitudes towards their international counterparts, with over half (52%) agreeing that they had good relations with nearby immigrant business people. A third felt that international migrants have as much right to trade and provide services as South Africans. And 38% agreed that South African and international migrant business people can work alongside each other.

Although no one found it acceptable to loot and burn down the businesses of international migrants, not all South African entrepreneurs were welcoming. Nearly half (48%) thought that only a specified number of immigrant businesses should be allowed to trade in their area and 39% that all immigrant businesses should be closed down. These negative opinions are similar to the attitudes of South Africans towards international migrants found in QoL 2013.[38] In QoL 2013, 38% of respondents said "all foreigners should be sent home, Gauteng is for South Africans only"; 44% that "legal foreigners are OK" and 18% that "all foreigners should be allowed to stay."[39] Thus, the attitudes of South African migrant entrepreneurs to their international counterparts may have more to do with general levels of hostility to international migrants in Johannesburg than to their specific status as entrepreneurs.

CONCLUSION

The opinions of South African migrant entrepreneurs demonstrate the complexity of attitudes and interactions and that South African entrepreneurs do not speak with one voice. Although a relatively high proportion of South Africans wanted to limit the rights of international migrants to do business, a substantial proportion enjoy positive and lucrative relationships with international migrant entrepreneurs.

Debates about international migration in South Africa often centre on the role of international migrant entrepreneurs who are seen to be more successful than their South African counterparts, squeezing them out of entrepreneurial spaces, particularly in townships. International migrant entrepreneurs are often the focus of xenophobic attacks. This survey challenges many commonly held opinions about the way that South African and international migrants establish and run their businesses. Importantly, it identifies the multiple relationships that exist between South African and international migrant entrepreneurs and shows that many of the challenges they face are shared:

- The policy environment that they operate in, particularly on a municipal level, is ambiguous and unstable.

- Possibly as a consequence, they face considerable challenges to their businesses from the state, including assault (both physical and verbal), confiscation of goods, demands for bribes, and harassment.

- Although their business premises should be relatively stable, the forcible removals of Operation Clean Sweep in 2013 demonstrate how vulnerable street traders are, even when they rent premises from the municipality.

- Most are entering the sector without previous business experience and without relevant skills and training.

- Access to capital is a problem and the formal banking sector appears to provide little or no support to informal sector entrepreneurs. Better access to affordable credit to start and expand their businesses would assist these entrepreneurs regardless of nationality.

- The businesses struggle with fierce competition in a crowded market. While the survey responses do not make it clear that reducing the number of informal sector entrepreneurs would solve this problem, there is conflict among entrepreneurs that does need to be addressed. Competition from large formal sector shops is equally challenging.

- There are many points at which the entrepreneurial activities of South African and international migrants intersect. South Africans buy supplies from immigrant businesses, learn from them and rent business premises to them.

While xenophobia is obviously an issue, not all South African entrepreneurs were opposed to the presence of international migrant entrepreneurs. Their attitudes to international migrants, regardless of economy activity, tended to mirror those of other South Africans in Johannesburg and Gauteng. One of the important findings of the survey is that participation in the informal sector does not necessarily put people in marginal economic positions. Interviewees, regardless of nationality, were likely to be earning more than other black Africans in the city. Many are also providing employment to other Johannesburg residents. They contribute to the tax base by buying from the formal sector. They pay rent to the municipality and private landlords. They therefore make contributions to their own households, their local communities and the government fiscus. Overall, the data suggests that it would be most fruitful to look at the common problems faced by entrepreneurs, regardless of their nationality, identify where best practices may enable them to develop profitable businesses equipped to employ more people, and empower them to contribute to the economic development of the city.

ENDNOTES

1   GCRO Quality of Life 2015 survey, www.gcro.ac.za\qol2015\

2   Bénit-Gbaffou. *A Political Landscape of Street Trader Organisations in Inner City Johannesburg*; Charman and Piper, "Xenophobia, Criminality and Violent Entrepreneurship; Crush et al., *Mean Streets*; Crush and Ramachandran, *Migrant Entrepreneurship, Collective Violence and Xenophobia in South Africa*; Gastrow and Amit, *Somalinomics.*

3   Judgment/LVS in the North Gauteng High Court, Pretoria, 19 September 2013, Case No: 16541/2013; Supreme Court of Appeal of South Africa Judgment, Case No: 48/2014.

4   Department of Home Affairs, Green Paper on International Migration, 21 June 2016, Government Gazette No. 40088, pp. 16-78.

5   Department of Trade and Industry, "A Draft Discussion Document Towards the National Informal Business Development Strategic Framework, Version 1" Pretoria, 2012.

6   Department of Trade and Industry, "National Informal Business Development Strategy" Pretoria, 2013, p. 24.

7   Ibid., p. 25.

8   "Foreign-Owned Businesses Hampering Rural Growth – DTI", *City Press* 10 October 2013.

9   "Spazas: Talking shop is good for business", *Mail and Guardian* 7 November 2014.

10 "Reveal Trade Secrets, Minister Tells Foreigners" *Business Day* 28 January 2015.

11 "Attacks on Foreigners Not Xenophobia: Committee" *News24* 10 July 2015. In mid-2015, President Jacob Zuma made claims to the African Union that there was no xenophobia in South Africa: C. du Plessis, "Zuma Denies Xenophobia in AU Discussion" *News24* 14 June 2015.

12 Bénit-Gbaffou, "In Quest for Sustainable Models of Street Trading Management"; Zack, "'Jeppe'".

13 "Police Proud of Work Around Inner-City 'Clean Up'" *Mail & Guardian* 1 November 2013.

14 "Claims of Collateral Damage as City Centre gets Massive Clean-Up" *The Star* 24 October 2013.

15 "Police Proud of Work."

16 Statistics South Africa (StatsSA), Census 2011, SuperCROSS.

17 "Growing Informal Sector Contributes 5% of GDP" *Business Report* 15 August 2014 (accessed 14 March 2015).

18 Statistics South Africa, *Survey of Employers and the Self-Employed, 2013* (Pretoria, 2014); StatsSA, "Press Statement: Survey of Employers and the Self-Employed (SESE), 2013" 14 August 2014. An informal business in the SESE survey is one which is not VAT registered and has fewer than five employees.

19 "Growing Informal Sector Contributes 5% of GDP".

20 For more information about the GCRO Quality of Life 2015 survey and access to data see: www.gcro. ac.za/qol/. See also Peberdy, *Informal Sector Enterprise and Employment in Gauteng*. For access to data from the GCRO 2009, 2011 and 2013 Quality of Life surveys see www.gcro.ac.za/qolviewer

21 Peberdy, *Informal Sector Enterprise and Employment in Gauteng*.

22 www.gcro.ac.za

23 Tawodzeraet al., *International Migrants and Refugees in Cape Town's Informal Economy*; Peberdy, *International Migrants in Johannesburg's Informal Economy*.

24 The survey was also extended by the GCRO to include international and South African migrants in other places in Gauteng; see Peberdy, "De-Bunking Myths"; Peberdy, "Locating the Informal Economy of the Gauteng City-Region".

25 Statistics South Africa, *Survey of Employers and the Self-Employed*.

26 Peberdy, *Selecting Immigrants*.

27 Ibid.

28 Ibid.

29 Peberdy, "A City on the Move."

30 Peberdy and Dinat, *Migration and Domestic Workers*; King, *Domestic Service in Post-Apartheid South Africa*.

31 Carsrud and Brännback, "Entrepreneurial Motivations"; Khosa and Kalitanyi, "Migration, Reasons,

Traits and Entrepreneurial Motivation"; Williams, "Entrepreneurs Operating in the Informal Economy"; Williams, "Motives of Off-the-Books Entrepreneurs"; Williams and Nadin, "Entrepreneurship and the Informal Economy".

32 Chen, "The Informal Economy: Definitions, Theories and Policies"; Heintz and Valodia, "Informality in Africa"; Skinner, "Street Trade in Africa."

33 Thompson," Risky Business and Geographies of Refugee Capitalism"; Fatoki and Patswawairi, "Motivations and Obstacles to Immigrant Entrepreneurship"; Mitchell, "Motives of Entrepreneurs"; Shane, Locke and Collins, "Entrepreneurial Motivation."

34 The mean score of each factor was calculated by multiplying the scale number by the number of respondents who had selected that rank (extremely important, important, neither, not important, not important at all). The sum for each rank was then added together and divided by the number of respondents (618 for international migrants or 310 for South Africans).

35 *Stokvels* are informal savings groups set up by people who are usually known to each other.

36 The personal and small business income tax thresholds set by the South African Revenue Services (SARS) for 2014/2015 was ZAR70,700 per annum. Respondents were not asked if they were registered with SARS for personal or small business income tax, or if they paid it where it was owed.

37 Statistics South Africa, *Census 2011*, SuperCROSS.

38 *www.gcro.ac.za/qolviewer/*

39 Ibid.

REFERENCES

1. Bénit-Gbaffou, C. (ed.). (2013). *A Political Landscape of Street Trader Organisations in Inner City Johannesburg, Post Operation Clean Sweep* (Johannesburg: CUBES and Wits School of Architecture and Planning).

2. Bénit-Gbaffou, C. (2015). "In Quest for Sustainable Models of Street Trading Management: Lessons for Johannesburg after Operation Clean Sweep" Technical Report, CUBES and School of Architecture and Planning. Wits University, Johannesburg.

3. Bracking, S. and Sachikonye, L. (2010). "Migrant Remittances and Household Wellbeing in Urban Zimbabwe" *International Migration* 48: 203-227.

4. Carsrud, A. and Brännback, M. (2011). "Entrepreneurial Motivations: What Do We Still Need to Know?" *Journal of Small Business Management* 49: 9-26.

5. Charman, A. and Piper, L. (2012). "Xenophobia, Criminality and Violent Entrepreneurship: Violence against Somali Shopkeepers in Delft South, Cape Town, South Africa" *South African Review of Sociology* 43: 81-105.

6. Chen, M. (2012). "The Informal Economy: Definitions, Theories and Policies" WIEGO Working Paper No. 1, Cambridge, MA and Manchester, UK.

7. Crush, J. and Pendleton, W. (2009). "Remitting for Survival: Rethinking the Development Potential of Remittances in Southern Africa" *Global Development Studies* 5: 1–28.

8. Crush, J. and Ramachandran, S. (2014). *Migrant Entrepreneurship, Collective Violence and Xenophobia in South Africa*. SAMP Migration Policy Series No. 67, Cape Town.

9. Crush, J., Chikanda, A. and Skinner, C. (eds.). (2015). *Mean Streets: Migration, Xenophobia and Informality in South Africa* (Ottawa, Cape Town and Waterloo: IDRC, ACC and SAMP).

10. Crush, J., Chikanda, A., Tawodzera, G. and Tengeh, R. (2015). *International Migrants and Refugees in Cape Town's Informal Economy*. SAMP Migration Policy Series No. 70, Cape Town.

11. Fatoki, O. (2012). "The Impact of Ethics on the Availability of Trade Credit to New Small and Medium Sized Enterprises (SMEs) in South Africa" *Journal of Social Sciences* 30: 21-29.

12. Fatoki, O. and Patswawairi, T. (2012). "The Motivations and Obstacles to Immigrant Entrepreneurship in South Africa" *Journal of Social Sciences* 32: 133-142.

13. Gastrow, V. and Amit, R. (2013). "Somalinomics: A Case Study on the Economics of Somali Informal Trade in the Western Cape" ACMS Research Report, Johannesburg.

14. Heintz, J. and Valodia, I. (2008). "Informality in Africa: A Review" WIEGO Working Paper No. 3, Cambridge, MA and Manchester, UK.

15. James, D. (2012). "Money-Go-Round: Personal Economies of Wealth, Aspiration and Indebtedness" *Africa* 82: 20-40.

16. Khosa, R. and Kalitanyi, V. (2015). "Migration, Reasons, Traits and Entrepreneurial Motivation of African Immigrant Entrepreneurs: Towards an Entrepreneurial Migration Progression" *Journal of Enterprising Communities: People and Place in the Global Economy* 9(2): 132-155.

17. King, A. (2012). *Domestic Service in Post-Apartheid South Africa: Deference and Disdain* (Farnham: Ashgate).

18. Makina, D. (2012). "Migration and Characteristics of Remittance Senders in South Africa" *International Migration* 51: e148-e158.

19. Makina, D. (2013). "Financial Access for Migrants and Intermediation of Remittances in South Africa" *International Migration* 51(s1): e133-147.

20. Maphosa, F. (2007). "Remittances and Development: The Impact of Migration to South Africa on Rural Livelihoods in Southern Zimbabwe" *Development Southern Africa* 24: 123-136.

21. Mashigo, P. and Schoeman, C. (2010). "Stokvels as an Instrument and Channel to Extend Credit to Poor Households in South Africa: An Inquiry" Policy Paper No. 19, University of Johannesburg, Johannesburg.

22. Mitchell, B. (2004). "Motives of Entrepreneurs: A Case Study of South Africa" *Journal of Entrepreneurship* 13: 167-183.

23. Peberdy, S. (2009). *Selecting Immigrants: National Identity and South Africa's Immigration Policies, 1910-2008* (Johannesburg: Wits University Press).

24. Peberdy, S. (2015). "Informal Sector Enterprise and Employment in Gauteng" GCRO Data Brief No. 6, GCRO, Johannesburg.

25. Peberdy, S. (2015). "A City on the Move" In Z. Asmal and G. Trangos (eds.), *Movement Johannesburg: An Urban Anthology* (Johannesburg and Cape Town: Designing South Africa and South African Cities Network), pp. 40-51.

26. Peberdy, S. (forthcoming) "De-Bunking Myths: Cross-Border Migrant and South African Informal-Sector Entrepreneurs in Gauteng" in F. Fourie (ed.) *Tackling Unemployment and Poverty in South Africa: The Contribution of the Informal Sector* (Cape Town: HSRC Press).

27. Peberdy, S. (forthcoming) "Locating the informal economy of the Gauteng City-Region" In K. Cheruiyot (ed.) *Economic Geographies of the Gauteng City-Region* (London: Springer).

28. Peberdy, S. and Dinat, N. (2010). *Migration and Domestic Workers: Worlds of Work, Health and Mobility in Johannesburg.* SAMP Migration Policy Series No. 40, Cape Town.

29. Radipere, N. (2012). "An Analysis of Local and Immigrant Entrepreneurship in the South African Small Enterprise Sector (Gauteng Province)" PhD Thesis, UNISA, Pretoria.

30. Radipere, S. and Dhliwayo, S. (2014). "An Analysis of Local and Immigrant Entrepreneurs in South Africa's SME Sector" *Mediterranean Journal of Social Sciences* 5: 189-198.

31. Shane, S., Locke, E. and Collins, C. (2003). "Entrepreneurial motivation" *Human Resource Management Review* 13: 257-279.

32. Skinner, C. (2008). "Street Trade in Africa: A Review" WIEGO Working Paper No. 5, Cambridge, MA and Manchester, UK.

33. Statistics South Africa (2014). Survey of employers and the self-employed, 2013. Statistical release P0726. Statistics South Africa: Pretoria.

34. Tevera, D. and Chikanda, A. (2009). "Development Impact of International Remittances: Some Evidence from Origin Households in Zimbabwe" *Global Development Studies* 5: 273-302.

35. Thompson, D. (2015). "Risky Business and Geographies of Refugee Capitalism in the Somali Migrant Economy of Gauteng, South Africa" *Journal of Ethnic and Migration Studies* 42(1): 120-135.

36. Verhoef, G. (2001). "Informal Financial Service Institutions for Survival: African Women and Stokvels in Urban South Africa, 1930-1998" *Enterprise and Society* 2: 259-296.

37. Williams, C. (2007). "Entrepreneurs Operating in the Informal Economy: Necessity or Opportunity Driven?" *Journal of Small Business and Entrepreneurship* 20: 309-320.

38. Williams, C. (2009). "The Motives of Off-the-Books Entrepreneurs: Necessity or Opportunity Driven?" *International Entrepreneurship and Management Journal* 5: 203-217.

39. Williams, C. and Nadin, S. (2010). "Entrepreneurship and the Informal Economy: An Overview" *Journal of Developmental Entrepreneurship* 15: 361-378.

40. Zack, T. (2015). "'Jeppe' – Where Low End Globalisation, Ethnic Entrepreneurialism and the Arrival City Meet" *Urban Forum* 26(2): 131-150.

MIGRATION POLICY SERIES

1   *Covert Operations: Clandestine Migration, Temporary Work and Immigration Policy in South Africa* (1997) ISBN 1-874864-51-9

2   *Riding the Tiger: Lesotho Miners and Permanent Residence in South Africa* (1997) ISBN 1-874864-52-7

3   *International Migration, Immigrant Entrepreneurs and South Africa's Small Enterprise Economy* (1997) ISBN 1-874864-62-4

4   *Silenced by Nation Building: African Immigrants and Language Policy in the New South Africa* (1998) ISBN 1-874864-64-0

27 *Mobile Namibia: Migration Trends and Attitudes* (2002) ISBN 1-919798-44-7

28 *Changing Attitudes to Immigration and Refugee Policy in Botswana* (2003) ISBN 1-919798-47-1

29 *The New Brain Drain from Zimbabwe* (2003) ISBN 1-919798-48-X

30 *Regionalizing Xenophobia? Citizen Attitudes to Immigration and Refugee Policy in Southern Africa* (2004) ISBN 1-919798-53-6

31 *Migration, Sexuality and HIV/AIDS in Rural South Africa* (2004) ISBN 1-919798-63-3

32 *Swaziland Moves: Perceptions and Patterns of Modern Migration* (2004) ISBN 1-919798-67-6

33 *HIV/AIDS and Children's Migration in Southern Africa* (2004) ISBN 1-919798-70-6

34 *Medical Leave: The Exodus of Health Professionals from Zimbabwe* (2005) ISBN 1-919798-74-9

35 *Degrees of Uncertainty: Students and the Brain Drain in Southern Africa* (2005) ISBN 1-919798-84-6

36 *Restless Minds: South African Students and the Brain Drain* (2005) ISBN 1-919798-82-X

37 *Understanding Press Coverage of Cross-Border Migration in Southern Africa since 2000* (2005) ISBN 1-919798-91-9

38 *Northern Gateway: Cross-Border Migration Between Namibia and Angola* (2005) ISBN 1-919798-92-7

39 *Early Departures: The Emigration Potential of Zimbabwean Students* (2005) ISBN 1-919798-99-4

40 *Migration and Domestic Workers: Worlds of Work, Health and Mobility in Johannesburg* (2005) ISBN 1-920118-02-0

41 *The Quality of Migration Services Delivery in South Africa* (2005) ISBN 1-920118-03-9

42 *States of Vulnerability: The Future Brain Drain of Talent to South Africa* (2006) ISBN 1-920118-07-1

43 *Migration and Development in Mozambique: Poverty, Inequality and Survival* (2006) ISBN 1-920118-10-1

44 *Migration, Remittances and Development in Southern Africa* (2006) ISBN 1-920118-15-2

45 *Medical Recruiting: The Case of South African Health Care Professionals* (2007) ISBN 1-920118-47-0

46 *Voices From the Margins: Migrant Women's Experiences in Southern Africa* (2007) ISBN 1-920118-50-0

47 *The Haemorrhage of Health Professionals From South Africa: Medical Opinions* (2007) ISBN 978-1-920118-63-1

48 *The Quality of Immigration and Citizenship Services in Namibia* (2008) ISBN 978-1-920118-67-9

49 *Gender, Migration and Remittances in Southern Africa* (2008) ISBN 978-1-920118-70-9

50 *The Perfect Storm: The Realities of Xenophobia in Contemporary South Africa* (2008) ISBN 978-1-920118-71-6

51 *Migrant Remittances and Household Survival in Zimbabwe* (2009) ISBN 978-1-920118-92-1

52 *Migration, Remittances and 'Development' in Lesotho* (2010) ISBN 978-1-920409-26-5

53 *Migration-Induced HIV and AIDS in Rural Mozambique and Swaziland* (2011) ISBN 978-1-920409-49-4

54 *Medical Xenophobia: Zimbabwean Access to Health Services in South Africa* (2011) ISBN 978-1-920409-63-0

55 *The Engagement of the Zimbabwean Medical Diaspora* (2011) ISBN 978-1-920409-64-7

56 *Right to the Classroom: Educational Barriers for Zimbabweans in South Africa* (2011) ISBN 978-1-920409-68-5

57 *Patients Without Borders: Medical Tourism and Medical Migration in Southern Africa* (2012) ISBN 978-1-920409-74-6

58 *The Disengagement of the South African Medical Diaspora* (2012) ISBN 978-1-920596-00-2

59 *The Third Wave: Mixed Migration from Zimbabwe to South Africa* (2012) ISBN 978-1-920596-01-9

60 *Linking Migration, Food Security and Development* (2012) ISBN 978-1-920596-02-6

61 *Unfriendly Neighbours: Contemporary Migration from Zimbabwe to Botswana* (2012) ISBN 978-1-920596-16-3

62 *Heading North: The Zimbabwean Diaspora in Canada* (2012) ISBN 978-1-920596-03-3

63 *Dystopia and Disengagement: Diaspora Attitudes Towards South Africa* (2012) ISBN 978-1-920596-04-0

64 *Soft Targets: Xenophobia, Public Violence and Changing Attitudes to Migrants in South Africa after May 2008* (2013) ISBN 978-1-920596-05-7

65 *Brain Drain and Regain: Migration Behaviour of South African Medical Professionals* (2014) ISBN 978-1-920596-07-1

66 *Xenophobic Violence in South Africa: Denialism, Minimalism, Realism* (2014) ISBN 978-1-920596-08-8

67 *Migrant Entrepreneurship Collective Violence and Xenophobia in South Africa* (2014) ISBN 978-1-920596-09-5

68 *Informal Migrant Entrepreneurship and Inclusive Growth in South Africa, Zimbabwe and Mozambique* (2015) ISBN 978-1-920596-10-1

69 *Calibrating Informal Cross-Border Trade in Southern Africa* (2015) ISBN 978-1-920596-13-2

70 *International Migrants and Refugees in Cape Town's Informal Economy* (2016) ISBN 978-1-920596-15-6

71 *International Migrants in Johannesburg's Informal Economy* (2016) ISBN 978-1-920596-18-7

72 *Food Remittances: Migration and Food Security in Africa* (2016) ISBN 978-1-920596-19-4

73 *Informal Entrepreneurship and Cross-Border Trade in Maputo, Mozambique* (2016) ISBN 978-1-920596-20-0

74 *Informal Entrepreneurship and Cross-Border Trade between Zimbabwe and South Africa* (2017) ISBN 978-1-920596-29-3

Printed in the United States
By Bookmasters